101 IDEAS TO SAVE PUBLIC CLOUD S

REDUCE CLOUD COMPUTING Cost

ABHINAV MITTAL
IT Cost Reduction Expert

INDIA • SINGAPORE • MALAYSIA

Notion Press

Old No. 38, New No. 6
McNichols Road, Chetpet
Chennai - 600 031

First Published by Notion Press 2019
Copyright © Abhinav Mittal 2019
All Rights Reserved.

ISBN 978-1-64546-815-8

Author's Note

Congratulations on buying your copy of **"Reduce Cloud Computing Cost – 101 Ideas to Save Millions in Public Cloud Spending."** I am delighted to know that like many of my clients, you have made a conscious choice to reduce wasteful spending in Information Technology.

Leading technology researchers suggest that worldwide public cloud spending is forecasted to touch USD 250 BN by 2020 with Amazon, Microsoft, and Google taking away significant market share. IaaS, PaaS, and SaaS are now preferred ways for building, testing, deploying, and using technology solutions. Indeed, public cloud computing has revolutionized the way IT services are delivered.

Before the public cloud, IT Cost was an issue of CIO and CFO. Developers were given technology resources they needed to code the application. Unless there was a scope change, they never had to worry about the cost of the solution. Budgeting was done once a year and projects capex was planned for a long time. These planned capacities had high buffers as no one wanted to go back to finance asking for more money.

Everything was going fine, till cloud computing came with the magic of "On-demand" resource provisioning. Developers were no longer limited by Infrastructure team on how much resources they were allotted, and Business users could buy whatever software they wanted from the Internet without IT ever finding out. Public cloud became a free rein where anyone with a credit card could do anything.

Today, this uncontrolled freedom for many companies resulted in larger than expected cloud bills. Lacking adequate governance, resources on the cloud have started costing more than those which are still on-premise. With rampant overprovisioning, 60% of companies acknowledge that a lot more needs to be done to get control of cloud costs.

Unlike a technology manual, My book 'Reduce Cloud Computing Cost – 101 Ideas to save millions in public cloud spending' offers 101 practical recommendations for technology professionals to source, tag, track and utilize IaaS, PaaS, SaaS resources on public cloud, thus governing sprawling cloud cost.

I hope you enjoy reading my book as much as I enjoyed writing it.

Do not forget "Buy what you use and use what you bought" the golden mantra to reduce IT Cost.

Share your comments or feedback with me.

Abhinav Mittal
IT Productivity Coach

in linkedin.com/in/mittalabhinav

⊛ abhinavmittal.com

✉ abhinav@abhinavmittal.com

🐦 abhinavmittal

May 2019

What Is Public Cloud Computing

A **computer** consists of 3 components to process data and perform calculations.

- **Hardware:** Electrical and Mechanical components such as a processor, memory, storage, communication ports etc.

- **System Software:** Set of instructions which are needed to control the Hardware.

- **Application Software:** Set of instructions which perform calculations and returns output based on a given input.

Pre-cloud days, one would need to buy large computers to run business applications. Owning hardware and software used to be a high capex activity, costing millions in refresh and maintenance. These computers (aka servers) would run from large facilities (aka datacentres) which were typically found near business premises.

With the advent of high-speed Internet, companies realized that they can now run the business applications from a distant server owned by a service provider without investing into their own. High-speed internet with few other technologies such as virtualization led to the creation of what we call public cloud computing.

Public Cloud Computing in simplistic terms means renting of hardware, system software, application software from a cloud services provider and running the same from the internet, instead of your own datacentre.

Most public cloud services fall into 3 categories (IaaS, PaaS and SaaS)

IaaS (Infrastructure as a Service) – is renting IT Hardware (servers, storage, networks) from a cloud provider for a pre-determined capacity or pay as go basis. IaaS helps companies grow the infrastructure as their business grows without requiring companies to invest in expensive on-premise hardware.

PaaS (Platform as a Service) – is renting cloud-based software services for developing, testing, delivering and managing software applications without developers bothering about setting up or managing the underlying infrastructure of network, servers, storage needed for application development.

SaaS (Software as a Service) – is renting software applications required by business users without user managing the underlying cloud infrastructure, or even individual application capabilities, with the possible exception of limited user-specific application configuration settings.

There is no doubt that cloud computing has improved the speed at which developers can write new applications. However, the ease of provisioning public cloud resources has left many companies struggling, as their total monthly costs are now spiraling out of control. Mentioned in my book are 101 ideas, which will help you to build long term cost controls while focusing on immediate reductions in the cost of your public cloud landscape.

101 IDEAS TO SAVE MILLIONS IN PUBLIC CLOUD SPENDING

1

Remove Unattached Cloud Storage

When VM (Virtual Machines) are stopped, storage volumes are not automatically deleted, and they continue to accrue charges. These unattached virtual hard disks (VHD's) keep consuming storage costs in public cloud since these disks are still considered operational by cloud providers. AWS by default sets DeleteOnTermination flag to false to avoid accidental deletion of data. Thus, an easy way to reduce cloud costs is to find and delete unattached volumes.

 # IaaS

 # Storage

2

Buy Right Storage Based on How Often and How Quickly You Need to Access the Data?

IaaS

Public cloud providers offer multiple kinds of storage pricing based on frequency required to access data. Storage costs Per GB/Month can go up by as much as 5 times between Cold long-term storage (Infrequently accessed data such as backups) vs Hot storage (Required for frequent access for business applications, dynamic websites or analytics). Since cloud vendors allow you to easily move data between these storage options, it makes sense to decide the right kind of storage to manage cloud costs.

Storage

3

Automatically Delete Storage Objects After An Expiry Date

Configure object lifecycle management policy to delete all non-required objects to reduce cloud storage costs. This is especially helpful for backup objects, which can be set for automatic deletion after they have reached their expiry dates.

IaaS

Storage

4

Rightsize Underutilized Storage Volumes

As there is no simple way to shrink storage volumes in the cloud, I recommend to periodically identify oversized volumes and then create a new rightsized volume to migrate the existing data. Better planning of storage requirements will avoid the cost of bigger unutilized storage volumes.

IaaS

Storage

Downgrade Storage Based on Throughput Required

You can reduce IaaS storage cost by monitoring the read-write access of volumes to check if throughput is low, then downgrade disk to lower IOPS (Input/output operations per second) disk to save cost.

laaS

Storage

6

Determine the Level of Redundancy Needed for Storage

Does all your data really need to be replicated thousands of kilometers away from the primary region? Plan your redundancy requirements wisely since redundancy in different geographies can be twice as expensive as local redundancy.

Iaas

Storage

Delete Old Snapshots

Companies use snapshots on storage to create recovery points for disaster recovery scenarios. In case systems are configured to take daily snapshots without deleting old snapshots, Cloud storage costs can grow multi-fold. Make sure to check stale snapshots and delete them to reduce storage cost.

IaaS

Storage

8

Manage Outbound Data Transfer Requests

In cloud, data transfer cost depends on the source and the destination of cloud servers. While inbound traffic is mostly free, providers tend to charge when you are transferring information between virtual private cloud, availability zones or external links. Try to compress data, perform data deduplication and do only incremental synchronization to save data transfer cost.

 # IaaS

 # Storage

Minimize Cross Geographies or Cross-Zone Data Transfers

When data moves across regions or countries, cloud providers consider it as making a long-distance phone call. If left unmonitored this can cost a huge amount. Try architecting your solution to limit the number of cloud provider regions the data needs to travel. Create a localized version of data store to save data transfer cost.

 # IaaS

 # Storage

10

Monitor Storage Pricing Tiers

Cloud companies use words "Over/Under" to specify tiered pricing on cloud storage. Those words mean, that there are specific levels in the cloud provider's pricing table, which you must reach, in order to get a lower pricing. Also remember that in tiered pricing your total purchase volumes do not automatically get a higher discount after reaching the next level. Be watchful on how you calculate the storage cost, since higher discounts are only applicable for the data above the previous threshold.

 # IaaS

 # Storage

Clean Up Incomplete Uploads from Storage

If your workload requests users to upload files, then there might be partial objects left in cloud storage which had been interrupted while uploading. Even a small percentage of incomplete uploads may end up wasting huge space. Clean up incomplete uploads to reduce the cost of storage.

laaS

Storage

12

Start and Stop VM's at Scheduled Times

Question the business requirements for keeping all the cloud workloads powered on all the time. You will realize that all VM's do not require to be run 24 × 7. Stop your VM's on non-working days like holidays and weekends to save cloud cost.

IaaS

Compute

Turn Off Non-Critical Testing VM's Overnight

Application developers spin new VM's for testing, however, they forget to power down these VM's before leaving home for the day. Turning off unused test VM's every night can save cloud cost.

 # IaaS

 # Compute

14

Centralize the VM Provisioning Process

Virtual Machine Provisioning privileges allows to control who is authorized to deploy and customize virtual machines in the cloud. Since each resource on public cloud comes at a cost. It is recommended to limit the number of people who have the ability to provision new computing resources. If required, institutionalize a change control procedure wherein cost implications of any new VM is reviewed prior to provisioning.

IaaS

Compute

15

Rightsize Virtual Machines

Continuously assess the utilization and efficiency of your computing resources. Determine VM's where Max CPU utilization is consistently less than 5% and Max RAM utilization is less than 20%. Once you identify underutilized resources, either reduce the cloud resources allotted to the instance or release overprovisioned resources, to save IT cost.

IaaS

Compute

16

Properly Terminate or Delete Unused Virtual Machines

 # IaaS

When terminating a VM, make sure to select the right option which removes both compute and storage. If you are just Stopping (AWS) or Deallocating (Azure) VM, the attached bootable volume will not be deleted and standard charges for storage volumes will keep getting applied. To fully stop incurring charges for unused VM make sure to Terminate (AWS) or Delete (Azure) VM's.

Compute

17

Kill Instances Stuck at Boot

Monitor your environment to track virtual machines which were launched but failed later in the launch process and therefore are not fully operational. Cloud providers charge for VM's when they are started which includes time taken to boot. To avoid wasteful cost, make sure that VM's stuck at the boot server is either manually terminated or forced into the operational state to avoid billing surprises.

IaaS

Compute

18

Kill Instances that Have Become Unresponsive

There might be instances where a VM gets stuck and becomes unavailable. Now if the stuck VM did not cause a disruption, no one will notice and there is a possibility that these Zombie VM's will keep occupying system resources, unless they are killed or forcefully shutdown. Keep monitoring your compute environment to kill such instances consuming cost.

IaaS

Compute

19

Use SPOT Instances/ Low Priority VM's for Temporary High-Performance Computing Workloads

 # IaaS

SPOT Instances allow you to save up to 90% of the cost when compared to On-Demand Instances. This is achieved by bidding for unused capacity in a cloud vendors data center. Since your Instance will be taken away when some else bids higher than you, it is recommended to use Low Priority VM's (Azure)/SPOT (AWS) instances only for applications which are prepared for an Instance interruption or where the job completion time is flexible and the work is distributed across many VM's.

Compute

20

Change Instance Families to New Ones

 # IaaS

Cloud providers offer many families of instance types, each family optimized for specific workload performance objectives. Each family has multiple instance types varying in the amount of CPU, memory resources etc. As technology evolves, cloud providers introduce new and more efficient instance types. In the newer instance types, even with the same CPU and memory, performance can be better due to advancements in underlying hardware and software. Thus, by moving to a newer instance family the processing activity could also take a shorter amount of time thereby reducing the overall cost of compute.

Compute

21

Shift VM's to Lower Cost Regions

Cost of Cloud resources varies a lot by region since cloud providers have to account for the cost of building and operating a data center. If latency, compliance and inter-zone data transfer cost is not an issue then choose to deploy services in the cheapest region to save cloud cost.

IaaS

Compute

22

Add End Date to Dev Instances

Developers often create compute instances for test/dev/demo purposes. They forget to delete them after development is complete. As a result, these dev instances keep getting charged. By specifying the expiration date for such virtual machines, they can be automatically deleted after expiry date so that you don't incur unnecessary cost.

laaS

Compute

23

Don't Rush to Buy Reserved Instances

As a best practice, RI should have a minimum utilization of 70% throughout the year for it to be cost effective. An unused reserved instance is a horrible deal, where on one hand you will have paid for the unused reservation and then you will most probably pay on-demand rates for another instance to take its place. It should take a minimum of 2–3 months to get some good data to take a decision. So, Start Pay as you go, and don't rush to purchase reserved instances until you get a firm understanding of your instance utilization.

 # IaaS

Compute

24

Avoid Expiry of Your Reserved Instance (AWS)

Don't miss the expiry date of your reserved instance. In case of AWS, after your 1–3 year term expires, your instance is billed at On-Demand rates, So make sure to purchase another Reserved Instance with the same specifications to keep getting RI discount. Check payment history in billing console to keep a track of due dates and payments made.

IaaS

Compute

25

Avoid Mismatched Reserved Instance RI (AWS)

In AWS, Reserved Instance discount is only provided when you have a running instance that matches the specifications (type, availability zone, platform, and tenancy) of your Reserved Instance. A mismatch in any of the specifications may lead to discount not being applied.

IaaS

Compute

26

Sell Unused AWS Reserved Instance on Marketplace

If your business requirements change and certain RI is no longer required, AWS allows its customers to sell unused Standard Reserved Instances to any potential buyers. However, do note that AWS charges a service fee of 12 percent of the total upfront price of each Standard Reserved Instance you sell in the Reserved Instance Marketplace.

IaaS

Compute

27

Exchange Azure Reserved VM Instance with New Azure VM Instances

Unlike AWS which allows exchange only for convertible RI's, Azure allows you to make a change to your reserved VM instances due to new requirements. Azure offers a prorated refund that covers the unused portion of your committed funds, which can then be applied to a new Azure RI without any penalty.

 # IaaS

Compute

28

Get a Refund on Azure Unused Reserved VM Instances

Azure allows you to cancel your reserved instance plan (up to $50,000 per year) at any time and request a direct, pro-rated refund (subject to an early termination fee of 12 percent).

laaS

Compute

29

Utilize Discounted Test/Dev Servers for Microsoft Visual Studio Customers

Microsoft Offers active Visual Studio standard subscribers to use Azure Dev/Test servers VM's with SQL Server, SharePoint Server, or other software that is normally billed at a higher rate, at a discounted rate. Discounted rate offered my microsoft for such servers is equal to the rate for a Linux virtual machine of the same size and type.

 # IaaS

Compute

Use Azure Hybrid Benefit for Microsoft Windows Server to Save Cost

 # IaaS

"Azure Hybrid Use Benefit" from Microsoft allows Microsoft customers having software assurance on their on-premise Windows Server Standard & Datacentre licenses to reduce the cost of running the same OS in Microsoft Azure public cloud. By only paying the compute rate for VM which is equal to the Linux rate Microsoft claims customers can save up to 40 percent on running Windows Server virtual machines in the cloud.

Compute

Go for Custom VM Sizing to Save Cost

Few cloud vendors (GCP) allow you to customize amounts of CPU and memory needed for your workload. By adding or removing the resources from a predefined standard template, You can right-size the compute environment thereby reducing cloud cost.

 # IaaS

 # Compute

Use Private IP's to Reduce Data Transfer Cost

Providers charges high data transfer cost with a public IP or Elastic IP. If possible use a private IP/Set up Virtual Private Cloud (VPC) endpoints to create a private connection between the VPC and another cloud provider, thus avoiding need to use the Internet and thereby significantly reducing data transfer charges.

laaS

Network

33

Release Elastic IP's (EIP's) When Instances are Terminated

An Elastic IP address (EIP) is a public IP address which is reachable from the internet. EIP's offer flexibility to application developers since they can be reassigned to different instances as developers' launch and terminate servers. Mostly Elastic IP's are offered free if they are being used by an instance. However, the provider does charge for each EIP that you reserve and do not use. Hence it is recommended to release an Elastic IP if you no longer need it and reduce cloud cost.

 # IaaS

 # Network

34

Use a Right Load Balancer

Cloud load balancers distribute workloads across multiple resources. Using a load balancer increases the availability of your applications. In AWS, cloud load balancers come in various flavors – Classic, Application, Network etc. While application load balancer (ALB) is priced lower than classic load balancer, be aware before switching, since ALB might not support all communication protocols or authentication needs which classic load balancer does. Make sure you understand traffic routing needs for your workload and select what is most appropriate for your application.

 # IaaS

 # Network

35

Remove or Reconfigure Idle Virtual Network Gateways

Microsoft Azure charges on an hourly basis for virtual network gateways. It is recommended to remove virtual network gateways have been idle for over 30 days or are no longer needed to reduce IaaS cost.

IaaS

Network

36

Monitor Utilization of AWS Direct Connect or Azure Express Route

Your company might have provisioned direct connections with Cloud Services provider (AWS direct connect or Azure Express route) during the cloud migration. These direct connections might no longer be in use or more likely, could be underutilized. Downgrade or remove these connections to save cost.

 # IaaS

 # Network

Refactor Code to Reduce Computing Needs

Determine how much compute resources are consumed while code is executing in a cloud server. Maybe the code is giving correct output, however, it might be inefficient and consuming unnecessary resources due to the presence of legacy functions which were required 10 years back, however, have no business relevance today. Refactoring such code to reduce the compute requirements can move this code to lower cost VM and thus save cost.

 # IaaS

Development

38

Buy Reserved Instances Only When Firm Demand is Known in Advance

IaaS

If you require a workload that needs to operate 24/7 and expect it to run over for the next 12 months, it is recommended to go for a reserved instance, which offers discount over On-Demand Instances. Reserved instance come at a discount since it is an upfront commitment. RI's are best suited for scenarios where you have a firm view of business demand and can thus plan for exact costs up front. As a thumb rule, you should plan for 50% – 70% of known capacity for a reserved instance.

Sourcing

39

Use Free Tiers Judiciously

Most cloud providers offer a free tier. These free tiers across multiple products are great for developers who want to test out capabilities before putting in credit card details. Utilizing free tiers is a wonderful way to learn about new offerings from cloud providers. Try multiple offerings and pay only when you have made a decision to go ahead with cloud offering beyond free quota.

 # IaaS

 # Sourcing

40

Provision for Minimum and Autoscale for Peaks

laaS

Unlike Pre-cloud days where companies needed to buy compute & storage capacities for peaks, Public cloud allows companies to provision resources for minimum and scale up for peak, adjusting to real-time demand. On-Demand provisioning of cloud resources is possible through autoscaling. Autoscaling is the heart of cloud computing as it allows companies to buy cloud resources as they need, with an ability to increase their compute environment only during moments of the surge.

Sourcing

41

Understand the Total Cost of Ownership (TCO) When Migrating to PaaS Database

PaaS

Each business environment is different. As seamless it might sound, still migrating an "in production self-managed database" to a "cloud provider managed database" will have some loss of functionality over a fully managed database. You might need to invest in professional services to detect any compatibility issues, unsupported features, new tasks and functionalities which need to be carried post migration to run a successful DBaaS. Plan migration project cost carefully to avoid nasty overruns.

Database

42

Understand the Total Cost of Ownership (TCO) for Running PaaS Database

 # PaaS

Account for cost of additional services which might be required for running an efficient Database as a Service. Services such as database monitoring & maintenance tools, service bus, active directory (or other authentication services) might not be included in the cost of DBaaS offering. While these added services are easy to provision in the cloud, however, all these increase the cost of running cloud Database.

Database

43

Review the HA Requirements When Using (Azure SQL) Managed Hosting in the Cloud

PaaS

Microsoft Azure SQL Database is a highly available database platform, which offers 99.99% of uptime SLA. Azure managed SQL DBaaS automatically handles – patching, backups, replication, failure detection in underlying hardware, software or network, deploying bug fixes, failovers, database upgrades, and other maintenance tasks. Hence you should revisit the HA needs and avoid additional spends.

Database

44

Use the Azure Hybrid Benefit in SQL to Reduce the Running Cost of SQL in the Managed Cloud

PaaS

Microsoft Azure Hybrid Benefit for SQL Server allows companies having software assurance on their on-premise SQL license to offset some of their Azure SQL cost when migrating SQL Server workloads to Azure cloud. Microsoft claims that savings can be around 30% extra when compared with running SQL on the cloud without Azure Hybrid Benefit.

Database

45

Understand Data Transfer Charges While Building Cloud Data Warehouse

 # PaaS

The pricing on cloud data warehouse can be totally unpredictable. Cost of data transfer activities which used to be ignored in case of on-premise setup, gets charged in the cloud. Make sure to account for the cost of activities like loading data, allocating instances, and creating clusters as all of these will incur access prices. Streaming and querying the data for visualization events will also increase the cost. Understand all costs before building a cloud data warehouse.

Database

46

Delete Temporary Database Snapshots or Copies

In on-premise world, DBA's would create temporary copies of the database to reproduce and diagnose faults. Since the on-premise storage always had excess capacity it did not matter. However, in a cloud environment, each copy of database when sitting on high performance compute environment can cost a lot of money. Hence it is advisable to move the backup database copies to low-cost storage or offline to save cost.

PaaS

Database

47

Optimize the Number of Pushes on PaaS Based Push Notification Service

 # PaaS

Push notification vendors charge on the number of notifications sent out. Unless your mobile app is the one heavily used by all users, the number of pushes might be a lot more than needed. To optimize the PaaS push notification cost, segment your audience and push notifications to only those users who have used the app in last one year.

Notifications

48

Use Containers to Reduce the Size and Running Time for Virtual Machines

 # PaaS

Containerization is an operating system-level virtualization method that simplifies application deployment by reducing the need for compute and storage requirements for virtual machines hosted in the cloud. In Hardware virtualization each VM takes up a lot of system resources, since each VM runs not just a full copy of an operating system, but a virtual copy of all the hardware that the operating system needs to run. With containers, instead of virtualizing the underlying virtual machine (VM), just the OS is virtualized. Which reduces the need to reproduce the operating system code, thus allowing a server to run multiple workloads with single operating system installation. Thereby making containers exceptionally light and low-cost choice over bulky VM's.

Containers

49

Use Namespaces to Establish Purpose and Ownership of Containers

PaaS

Using namespaces (akin to a family name) is a way of dividing a cluster into several virtual clusters. These virtual clusters can then be associated with specific departments, services or applications to allocate resources, establish ownership and determine purpose (dev/test) for which the pods have been created. This helps in tracking application cost.

Containers

Set Quotas on Your Container Pods

When several users or teams share a cluster with a fixed number of nodes, one team could use more than its fair share of resources thereby impacting other team's work. Applying resource quota on namespaces limits, number of objects which can be created in that namespace and, amount of compute that may be used by resources in the project.

PaaS

Containers

51

Monitor Pod's Resource Utilization

Regular monitoring of resource utilization across pods is key to keep cost low in a container environment. It is suggested to use dashboards which provide information on the current level of compute, memory, network and storage resource consumption, with their cost metrics. You can also use tools like Grafana and Prometheus to periodically check resource utilization by each pod.

PaaS

Containers

52

Automate Pod Downsizing

Use a Vertical Pod Autoscaler (VPA) to automatically downsize the underutilized Pod when developers forget to do so. VPA can track resource (CPU and memory) of the Pod and reset it's limit to free any excess provisioned capacity.

PaaS

Containers

53

Increase Duration of Cached Media

Content Delivery Network are designed to send media files across geographically diverse locations faster, by caching information on servers closest to each user. Cloud providers charge by the amount of data that is transmitted from a specific location, with each location having its own rate. You can reduce the bandwidth consumption by increasing the time media files are kept in cache. Thereby reducing the times a browser fetches information from CDN, thus reducing CDN cost.

PaaS

CDN

Optimize Website for Quicker Load Times

Reduce page load times, by designing your websites appropriately thus ensuring minimal roundtrip requests are made to the backend for content retrieval. This can further reduce CDN cost.

PaaS

CDN

55

Rightsize Images

Limit image size on your websites. Identify image formats and delivery, based on devices of your users. Poster quality, Multi megapixel images are not required if your primary audience is mobile based. By rightsizing your images you consume less bandwidth, thus reducing your CDN cost, without compromising on user experience.

 # PaaS

 # CDN

56

User Serverless Computing for Running Pilots and Proof of Concepts with Fixed Budgets

 # PaaS

For pilots or projects whose fate is unknown, use serverless computing to keep cost in control. Serverless applications let developers run code without provisioning or managing servers. Serverless computing eliminates developers from infrastructure management tasks such as server or cluster provisioning, patching, operating system maintenance, and capacity provisioning. With serverless computing cloud vendor, charges are based on the actual amount of resources consumed by an application, and developers do not have to reserve resources and pay for a fixed amount of bandwidth or number of servers.

Serverless Computing

57

Appropriately Decide on the Maximum Execution Time of the Serverless Function

Developers tend to set the execution time of their function to a large number. If this function is waiting for external input, this will add to execution time thereby adding to cost of running a serverless function. When using serverless it is recommended to plan timeouts carefully as each second of function running is an additional cost.

 # PaaS

Serverless Computing

58

Compute the Total Cost of Ownership for Serverless

 # PaaS

The total cost of serverless computing is more than just compute (CPU and RAM). It is likely that for your application API requests, storage and networking could drive up additional cost. Serverless applications tend to be heavy on API calls. If your app transmits a lot of data outside the cloud providers region, plan carefully before using Serverless apps. Use serverless for apps which have predictable usage. Include the cost of migration into TCO as, any refactoring to serverless can burn a big hole in the pocket.

Serverless Computing

59

Optimize Payload of Amazon Kinesis Data Stream

Amazon bills the Kinesis data stream per 25 KB payload unit. Even though each of your record might be just 400 bytes but Amazon counts each PUT record as 25 KB, hence for ingesting two records of 800 bytes total you will end up paying for 2 units (50 KB). Wasting a lot of space! To save cost when using Amazon Kinesis Data Streams, it is recommended to compress and aggregate several messages until you use full 25 KB payload unit.

PaaS

Data Stream Processing

Delete Obsolete Records Before Migrating to Cloud Active Directory

60

Clean your on-premise Microsoft Active Directory before migrating to cloud-based Azure AD, since on-premise might contain massive amounts of duplicate, unnecessary, or outdated computer/user objects. Try reducing forests and obsolete records which will reduce the cost of your cloud-based active directory.

PaaS

Active Directory

61

Centralize SaaS Sourcing

Multiple businesses buying the same SaaS products on their own only helps the product vendor. While SaaS products offer ease of purchase, Users may not get volume discounts which are only possible when quantities are combined into a single transaction. Hence it is recommended to centralize all SaaS purchases to get discounted pricing.

 # SaaS

 # Sourcing

62

Do Not Buy the Most Expensive, All-Inclusive Software Bundle

SaaS

Unbundle product offering from the software provider. Profile internal users to understand features/modules/functionalities they really use. Not all users need all the products from software providers most expensive suit. Create user profiles, combine products, group features, and buy only the variants which have proven useful for business. SaaS vendors always have upgrade options. If you miss a module now, you can buy it later.

Sourcing

63

Include Options to Reduce the Volume (True Down)

During the contract negotiation, include the contractual clause which allows you to reduce the subscription volumes during the contract duration. This is especially helpful in case you end up with higher than needed license numbers, wrongly predicted at the time of contract renewal.

 # SaaS

 # Sourcing

64

Lock Future Pricing on Additional Licenses (True Up)

When negotiating a high-volume contract, fix the unit price for any additional licenses at a unit price no higher than the original contract. Fixing unit prices will ensure that you are able to supply the same software to more business users without the need to justify any unwarranted increases in the software cost.

SaaS

Sourcing

65

Start Subscription Payments Only at the Start of Usage

If your product is having long implementation time, then negotiate to delay the payment for SaaS subscriptions till go live when all users are onboard. Without an agreement on the start date of the subscription, you will end up paying for software without any usage benefit.

SaaS

Sourcing

66

Freeze Yearly Inflation Increases on Support Cost

Some vendors charge for yearly increases in SaaS support cost based on inflation. You can negotiate such yearly increases to once in 2–3 years and baseline any increases on local inflation index to keep support cost in control.

SaaS

Sourcing

Review Your Support Needs for SaaS Software

67

The support required for a SaaS product is likely to be lower as there are limits to which product can be configured or customized. While vendors will like to push for the most expensive and most prompt support plan. You need to review the cost of getting immediate, highest SLA vendor support with downtime risk business is willing to take and then decide if you can lower the support plan to save SaaS cost.

 # SaaS

 # Sourcing

Know the Notice Needed for Contract Termination

Stopping the payment at anniversary does not mean that the contract is legally terminated. Many SaaS vendor require you to inform them up to 3 months in advance if you need to stop the contract at will. If you are planning to switch or drop a SaaS product, make sure to inform vendor early or budget for termination fees.

 # SaaS

 # Sourcing

Remove the Autorenewal Clause from the Contract

Most SaaS vendors have autorenewal clause in their contract. While the autorenewal clause ensures continuity of service, However it also takes away any negotiation leverage for future purchases. To keep vendor interested in your company's business, it is advisable to replace autorenewal clause with "renewal notice" clause under which vendor can issue a non-binding renewal notice up to 120 days in advance so you get to decide if it is worth continuing with the SaaS product.

 # SaaS

Sourcing

70

Change the Default Autorenewal Term

 # SaaS

SaaS vendors can be sneaky, they understand the busy legal executives do not have time to decipher fine print of each line in SaaS contract. Few SaaS contracts have autorenewal term set to a period of the 1st contract. Now if your 1st contract was for 3 years and the same was on auto-renewal for next 3 years, you might be stuck with the vendor. Which is an unpleasant situation in case your business wants to switch or drop the product? Make sure the autorenewal term is set to no more than 1 year to avoid legal hassles at the time of contract termination.

Sourcing

Negotiate ZERO Penalties for Overage Fees

 # SaaS

In a SaaS product, Vendor may allow you to activate more users beyond your entitlement, and automatically charge higher for those extra users. Thus resulting into unplanned licence cost called as overage. When negotiating a SaaS contract, challenge vendor to be transparent with overage metrics, have ZERO penalties and 90-day time window for validation of any overage charges.

Sourcing

72

Know Product Usage Limitations

SaaS products which claim unlimited usage may cap the usage under "Fair use" terms. Before buying into SaaS solution make sure to check for limits on storage, backup frequency, days of data retention, data transfer, and record keeping limits. In case your business has peculiar needs, document them in the contract to avoid any surprise charges.

SaaS

Sourcing

73

Negotiate Costs for Indirect Access

Many SaaS vendors have started charging for users/devices which are indirectly modifying data in their SaaS application. If not negotiated at the time of original purchase and discovered during a vendor audit, these Indirect users can lead to a significant increase in the cost of SaaS software. Hence when negotiating a SaaS contract make sure vendor clearly articulates what kind of indirect use is allowed, and what is not.

 # Saas

 # Sourcing

Negotiate SLA Breach Penalties

74

SaaS

SaaS provider SLA and penalties are full of exceptions. Hence while negotiating SaaS contract it is important to agree a SLA violation penalty at minimum 100% of the monthly subscription fees, if the system uptime falls to 95% (36 hours per month) or below. Not negotiating proper SLA is a sure way to pay for SaaS solution even if it did not work properly.

Sourcing

75

Negotiate Cost of Testing & Dev Instances

 # SaaS

For Enterprise applications like Salesforce, SAP, Oracle on SaaS, it is likely that you would need Test/Dev or Sandbox instances on the cloud. There are no industry standards here, each vendor has his own way of pricing the Sandbox environment. Negotiate hard with your SaaS provider for non-production instances as these test/dev instances need not run 24 × 7 and are used by limited users. As a thumb rule, you should start negotiations for text/dev from zero.

Sourcing

76

Agree on Licence Swap with Unused Licenses

Few vendors offer a choice to exchange the existing subscriptions for another product of the same value within the original order at the time of yearly renewal. This option is helpful as it allows you to avoid shelfware while retaining the negotiated discounts with SaaS provider.

SaaS

Sourcing

77

Time Your Negotiations

For most sales people, the last quarter in their fiscal year is when they close most deals (To meet yearly bonus targets). Hence your ability to more discount goes up in last quarter/ last month of the fiscal year of vendor where when sales people are likely to be more flexible in making concessions.

 # SaaS

 # Sourcing

Cancel Before the Expiry of the Trial If You Don't Intend to Continue with SaaS Product

SaaS

Few SaaS providers automatically convert from trial to a paid version after the trial period ends. Now if you entered your credit card details while taking a trial, you may get billed if you have not canceled the trial by explicitly informing the vendor. Avoid bill shock by timely canceling the trial.

Sourcing

79

Use All the Freebies That Come with Visual Studio Subscription

Read the fine print of SaaS software agreement to understand all the freebies that come with your SaaS subscription. As an example, Microsoft Visual Studio Enterprise subscription offers – 25 users Office 365 Developer subscription and 6 months subscription of LinkedIn learning. All of which could go waste if not used before the expiry of visual studio subscription.

SaaS

Sourcing

80

Use All the Freebies That Come with Office 365 Subscription

 # SaaS

You can reduce the cost of Microsoft office installations on multiple devices as popular variants of Microsoft Office 365 subscription allow a licensed user to install 5 copies of Microsoft office in PC or Mac. This effectively means you do not need to buy additional copy of popular Microsoft products (Word, Excel and powerpoint) for your home computers.

Sourcing

81

Remove Users Who Have Left the Company

Review the user license allocations at least once a month to identify and remove users who have left the company or moved to different roles. Monthly mapping of active users against available licenses ensures your company does not end up buying extra subscriptions for ghost users.

SaaS

Usage Monitoring

82

Remove Users Who Have Not Used the Application in the Last 90 Days

SaaS

Users stop using the software if it does not meet their business needs. However, they do not inform IT to revoke access, thus consuming licenses. It is recommended to revoke SaaS licenses from users who have not used the product for 30–60–90 days and repurpose the same license to real users thereby reducing the need to buy extra licenses.

Usage Monitoring

83

Showback User Level SaaS Software Usage Report

Showback is a way to inform business heads about those users in their team who are using SaaS software. Since many SaaS licenses are activated for named users, it is recommended to issue a monthly SaaS utilization report. By naming the users for each SaaS software, Business heads will be able to take action and advise any revocations, thus keeping SaaS cost in control.

 # SaaS

Usage Monitoring

84

Remove Redundant Applications

In companies which had decentralized IT or went through merger and acquisition process, it is likely that there will be redundant SaaS applications. Popular ones in this category are video conferencing, online storage, project management tools, etc. To optimize software cost it is recommended to consolidate and limit the applications which offer the same functionality.

SaaS

Portfolio Rationalization

85

Remove Duplicate Licenses for the Same User

Sometimes users have on-premise installation and SaaS access of the same application. Unless the vendor allows for dual usage rights, this can become a problem since the company ends up paying twice for the same user. Scan computers for product installations and remove or revoke non-required license to save SaaS cost.

 # SaaS

Portfolio Rationalization

Consolidate IaaS Buying Accounts

In a large company, there is a high likelihood that many users would have created their own accounts on AWS/Azure/GCP or other cloud providers. These non-centralized accounts cause users to miss on discounts associated with volume pricing and reservations. A combined view of your cost and usage is helpful in getting full visibility into cloud cost thus optimizing overall cloud spending.

Governance

Sourcing

87

Plan Full TCO (Total Cost of Ownership) for Applications

Carefully consider all aspects of your cloud application when planning the budget. Make sure to account for costs related to Testing, Development, Pre-production, Staging instances, Cloud data transfers, Additional bandwidths, Server licenses etc. Remain watchful as missing on any of these can spring up huge costs in final bill from the cloud provider.

Governance

Financial Management

88

Tag Your Assets

Tagging of cloud resources is critical for governance of cloud investments. A tag is an organization specific metadata label that you assign to a cloud resource for purposes of cost allocation, tracking of ownership, use and expected duration of cloud asset. There are few core tags that should be present on any cloud-based workload such as Owner, Cost Center, Project, Application, and Purpose. A good tagging discipline will bring business accountability and financial transparency for managing cloud cost.

 # Governance

 # Financial Management

89

Create a Cloud Resource Tagging Policy

 # Governance

A cloud resource tagging policy ensures tags accurately reflect your organizational structure and follow standardized naming convention (e.g. use of Small case/Upper case). This is especially helpful when tags are created by multiple teams. Tagging policy also mandates which tags must be defined when a new resource is created. A good tagging policy is a must to establish accountability and manage deployment sprawl in a large cloud computing setup.

Financial Management

90

Chargeback Cloud Cost to Users

 # Governance

Chargeback is measuring the amount of cloud cost incurred in providing a business service and then allocating the same cost to the departments and business units requesting that IT service. Chargebacks are especially helpful if the organization allows anyone to provision cloud resources which are paid from a central cost pool. Chargeback makes service consumers aware of the cost of cloud, which then help in establishing business accountability, controlling escalating cloud cost and improving decision making on effective usage of IT resources.

Financial Management

91

Set Budget Alerts on Cloud Consumption

Budget alerts assist in controlling cost by triggering alert notifications for billing administrators, managers, finance teams, and other users after actual or forecasted costs exceed a percentage of the budget or a specified amount. Budgets can be configured easily in AWS, Azure, and GCP. Knowing how much is left to be spent against what was budgeted is a good practice to keep cloud cost in control.

Governance

Financial Management

92

Set Department Quotas

By setting a per department Quota, you can prevent wasteful resource usage in your cloud environment. For example, a quota can limit the number of virtual servers allowed for users in the testing group or issue alerts when a department usage reaches a fixed threshold of the quota.

Governance

Financial Management

Review Cost at the End of Your Billing Cycle

 # Governance

Make sure you understand each line of your cloud providers monthly bill. Compare bill with cloud services that developers have provisioned. Exceeding free tier, over-provisioned resources, inter-zone data transfer cost, usage charges for exceeding access limits of long term storage or any unusual traffic for a specific computing resource are common culprits for billing surprises. Raise support tickets or call support center to seek explanations for any anything which is not clear. Knowing what you are paying for, is a key to control cloud cost.

Financial Management

94

Measure – IaaS Underutilization of Committed Capacities

Knowing how much ideal capacity is there in cloud provisioned services such as Reserved Instances, Virtual Machines, Storage Volumes, Load Balancers, Express routes etc. Helps in identifying cloud wastage. By aggregating all the over-provisioned & unused capacities, you will discover opportunities to resize the cloud environment and thereby reducing cloud cost.

 # Governance

Metrics

95

Measure – Overall Budget vs Actual Cloud Cost

The 1st metric that should be tracked to control cloud cost is budget vs actual cost of services provided by a cloud provider. When monitored every month this number will form the baseline for executive reporting and help management understand the overall cost of using public cloud computing.

 # Governance

 # Metrics

96

Measure – Application Wise Budgeted vs Actual vs Forecasted Cost

 # Governance

Even though it is complex to estimate demand for a new application, having a metric on cost baseline per application is better than having none. Request your business to forecast demand and then developers to give an overview of how much will be cost of running compute, occupying storage, networking, and data transfers across zones during development and production. Compare this forecast against actuals every month to take a decision on the financial viability of the cloud project.

Metrics

97

Measure – Cloud Cost Per Department

If there are multiple people across departments who are authorized to provision cloud resources, then it is imperative to measure cloud consumption per department. Measuring cost per department will enable the IT team to establish accountability and have a transparent discussion with business team sponsoring a project. It will also help in tracking if cloud spend is recorded incorrectly in unrelated departments.

 # Governance

 # Metrics

98

Measure – Cloud Cost Per Provisioned Service

Measuring cloud spends for each service provisioned in public cloud will help you determine how much storage, compute, network, and platform services are being currently used per cloud service provider. Knowing the services, being bought across providers, will help you reduce cost if there are cheaper choices available from alternate cloud providers.

 # Governance

 # Metrics

99

Measure – Cost of Prod/Test/Dev Resources

Measuring the cost consumed by production, testing and development environments will enable you to determine, opportunities to reduce cost by moving test/prod/dev to low cost or on demand machines which need not run 24 × 7 + weekends.

Governance

Metrics

100

Enthuse Collaboration Between Technology and Finance

 # Governance

Enterprises, where IT, business, and finance talk to each other, get more discounts and are better at perfecting cloud spending. By breaking the Organization's silos and being transparent about technology requirements, cloud cost structures, and approved budgets, companies can optimize costs better. This needs some education on finance team as they will need to develop an understanding of what makes up the cost of engineering solutions in the cloud and, IT engineers appreciating how finance accounts for cost of IT. When engineers do coding with cost consciousness they become efficient in developing cost-efficient cloud solutions.

All

101

Act to Save Cloud Cost

Ideas to reduce cloud cost can be helpful only when you act. There will be a time in every organization when someone will be looking for ideas to cut wasteful cloud spending. Apply any of the 100 ideas shared above to start saving cloud cost.

 # Governance

 # All

101 Ideas to Save Millions in Public Cloud Spending

Implementation Checklist:

IaaS

☐ Remove Unattached Cloud Storage

☐ Buy Right Storage Based on How Often and How Quickly You Need to Access the Data?

☐ Automatically Delete Storage Objects After An Expiry Date

☐ Rightsize Underutilized Storage Volumes

☐ Downgrade Storage Based on Throughput Required

☐ Determine the Level of Redundancy Needed for Storage

☐ Delete Old Snapshots

☐ Manage Outbound Data Transfer Requests

☐ Minimize Cross Geographies or Cross-Zone Data Transfers

☐ Monitor Storage Pricing Tiers

☐ Clean Up Incomplete Uploads from Storage

☐ Start and Stop VM's at Scheduled Times

☐ Turn Off Non-Critical Testing VM's Overnight

☐ Centralize the VM Provisioning Process

☐ Rightsize Virtual Machines

☐ Properly Terminate or Delete Unused Virtual Machines

☐ Kill Instances Stuck at Boot

☐ Kill Instances that Have Become Unresponsive

☐ Use SPOT Instances/Low Priority VM's for Temporary High-Performance Computing Workloads

- [ ] Change Instance Families to New Ones
- [ ] Shift VM's to Lower Cost Regions
- [ ] Add End Date to Dev Instances
- [ ] Don't Rush to Buy Reserved Instances
- [ ] Avoid Expiry of Your Reserved Instance (AWS)
- [ ] Avoid Mismatched Reserved Instance RI (AWS)
- [ ] Sell Unused AWS Reserved Instance on Marketplace
- [ ] Exchange Azure Reserved VM Instance with New Azure VM Instances
- [ ] Get a Refund on Azure Unused Reserved VM Instances
- [ ] Utilize Discounted Test/Dev Servers for Microsoft Visual Studio Customers
- [ ] Use Azure Hybrid Benefit for Microsoft Windows Server to Save Cost
- [ ] Go for Custom VM Sizing to Save Cost
- [ ] Use Private IP's to Reduce Data Transfer Cost
- [ ] Release Elastic IP's (EIP's) When Instances are Terminated
- [ ] Use a Right Load Balancer
- [ ] Remove or Reconfigure Idle Virtual Network Gateways
- [ ] Monitor Utilization of AWS Direct Connect or Azure Express Route
- [ ] Refactor Code to Reduce Computing Needs
- [ ] Buy Reserved Instances Only When Firm Demand is Known in Advance
- [ ] Use Free Tiers Judiciously
- [ ] Provision for Minimum and Autoscale for Peaks

PaaS

☐ Understand the Total Cost of Ownership (TCO) When Migrating to PaaS Database

☐ Understand the Total Cost of Ownership (TCO) for Running PaaS Database

☐ Review the HA Requirements When Using (Azure SQL) Managed Hosting in the Cloud

☐ Use the Azure Hybrid Benefit in SQL to Reduce the Running Cost of SQL in the Managed Cloud

☐ Understand Data Transfer Charges While Building Cloud Data Warehouse

☐ Delete Temporary Database Snapshots or Copies

☐ Optimize the Number of Pushes on PaaS Based Push Notification Service

☐ Use Containers to Reduce the Size and Running Time for Virtual Machines

☐ Use Namespaces to Establish Purpose and Ownership of Containers

☐ Set Quotas on Your Container Pods

☐ Monitor Pod's Resource Utilization

☐ Automate Pod Downsizing

☐ Increase Duration of Cached Media

☐ Optimize Website for Quicker Load Times

☐ Rightsize Images

☐ User Serverless Computing for Running Pilots and Proof of Concepts with Fixed Budgets

☐ Appropriately Decide on the Maximum Execution Time of the Serverless Function

☐ Compute the Total Cost of Ownership for Serverless

☐ Optimize Payload of Amazon Kinesis Data Stream

☐ Delete Obsolete Records Before Migrating to Cloud Active Directory

SaaS

☐ Centralize SaaS Sourcing

☐ Do Not Buy the Most Expensive, All-Inclusive Software Bundle

☐ Include Options to Reduce the Volume (True Down)

☐ Lock Future Pricing on Additional Licenses (True Up)

☐ Start Subscription Payments Only at the Start of Usage

☐ Freeze Yearly Inflation Increases on Support Cost

☐ Review Your Support Needs for SaaS Software

☐ Know the Notice Needed for Contract Termination

☐ Remove the Autorenewal Clause from the Contract

☐ Change the Default Autorenewal Term

☐ Negotiate ZERO Penalties for Overage Fees

☐ Know Product Usage Limitations

☐ Negotiate Costs for Indirect Access

☐ Negotiate SLA Breach Penalties

☐ Negotiate Cost of Testing & Dev Instances

☐ Agree on Licence Swap with Unused Licenses

- [ ] Time Your Negotiations
- [ ] Cancel Before the Expiry of the Trial If You Don't Intend to Continue with SaaS Product
- [ ] Use All the Freebies That Come with Visual Studio Subscription
- [ ] Use All the Freebies That Come with Office 365 Subscription
- [ ] Remove Users Who Have Left the Company
- [ ] Remove Users Who Have Not Used the Application in the Last 90 Days
- [ ] Showback User Level SaaS Software Usage Report
- [ ] Remove Redundant Applications
- [ ] Remove Duplicate Licenses for the Same User

Governance

- [ ] Consolidate IaaS Buying Accounts
- [ ] Plan Full TCO (Total Cost of Ownership) for Applications
- [ ] Tag Your Assets
- [ ] Create a Cloud Resource Tagging Policy
- [ ] Chargeback Cloud Cost to Users
- [ ] Set Budget Alerts on Cloud Consumption
- [ ] Set Department Quotas
- [ ] Review Cost at the End of Your Billing Cycle
- [ ] Measure – IaaS Underutilization of Committed Capacities
- [ ] Measure – Overall Budget vs Actual Cloud Cost

- ☐ Measure – Application Wise Budgeted vs Actual vs Forecasted Cost

- ☐ Measure – Cloud Cost Per Department

- ☐ Measure – Cloud Cost Per Provisioned Service

- ☐ Measure – Cost of Prod/Test/Dev Resources

- ☐ Enthuse Collaboration Between Technology and Finance

- ☐ Act to Save Cloud Cost